A Guide for Using

Across Five Aprils

in the Classroom

Based on the novel written by Irene Hunt

This guide written by **Dona Herweck Rice**

Teacher Created Materials, Inc.
6421 Industry Way
Westminster, CA 92683
www.teachercreated.com
©1999 Teacher Created Materials, Inc.
Reprinted, 2003
Made in U.S.A.
ISBN 1-57690-333-8

Edited by
David Cook

Illustrated by
Blanca Apodaca

Cover Art by
Dennis Carmichael

Table of Contents

Introduction 3

Sample Lesson Plans 4

About the Author 5

Book Summary 6

Before the Book (Prereading Activities) 7

Vocabulary Lists 8

Vocabulary Activity Ideas 9

Section I (*Chapters 1–3*) 10
- ❖ Quiz Time
- ❖ Hands-on Project—Vegetable Garden
- ❖ Cooperative Learning Activity—Understanding Dialects
- ❖ Curriculum Connection—History: Fort Sumter
- ❖ Into Your Life—Reader's Response Journals

Section II (*Chapters 4 and 5*) 15
- ❖ Quiz Time
- ❖ Hands-on Project—My Annex
- ❖ Cooperative Learning Activity—Important People of the Civil War
- ❖ Curriculum Connection—Social Studies: Map It Out
- ❖ Into Your Life—Political Cartoons

Section III (*Chapters 6 and 7*) 20
- ❖ Quiz Time
- ❖ Hands-on Project—Civil War Cornbread
- ❖ Cooperative Learning Activity—Helping Hands
- ❖ Curriculum Connection—Language Arts: What's New, Friend?
- ❖ Into Your Life—Growing Up

Section IV (*Chapters 8 and 9*) 25
- ❖ Quiz Time
- ❖ Hands-on Project—Nourishment
- ❖ Cooperative Learning Activity—Barn Raising
- ❖ Curriculum Connection—Math: How Big Should We Make It?
- ❖ Into Your Life—Respect

Section V (*Chapters 10–12*) 30
- ❖ Quiz Time
- ❖ Hands-on Project—Three Important Events
- ❖ Cooperative Learning Activity—Debate
- ❖ Curriculum Connection—Math: Civil War Casualties
- ❖ Into Your Life—In My Own Backyard

After the Book (*Postreading Activities*)
- Any Questions? 35
- Book Report Ideas 36
- Research Ideas 37

Culminating Activity 38

Unit Test Options 42

Bibliography of Related Reading 45

Answer Key 46

Introduction

A good book can touch our lives like a good friend. Within its pages are words and characters that can inspire us to achieve our highest ideals. We can turn to it for companionship, recreation, comfort, and guidance. It can also give us a cherished story to hold in our hearts forever.

In *Literature Units*, great care has been taken to select books that are sure to become good friends.

Teachers who use this unit will find the following features to supplement their own valuable ideas.

- Sample Lesson Plans
- Prereading Activities
- Biographical Sketch and Illustration of the Author
- Book Summary
- Vocabulary Lists and Suggested Vocabulary Ideas
- Chapters grouped for study, with each section including a

  —quiz

  —hands-on project

  —cooperative learning activity

  —cross-curricular connection

  —extension into the reader's own life

- Postreading Activities
- Book Report Ideas
- Research Ideas
- Culminating Activity
- Three Different Options for Unit Tests
- Bibliography of Related Reading
- Answer Key

We are confident that this unit will be a valuable addition to your planning, and we hope that as you use our ideas, your students will increase the circle of "friends" they have in books!

Sample Lesson Plans

Each of the lessons suggested below can take from one to several days to complete.

Lesson 1
- Introduce and complete some or all of the prereading activities (page 7).
- Read "About the Author" with your students (page 5).
- Introduce the vocabulary for Section 1 (page 8).

Lesson 2
- Read chapters 1–3. As you read, note the vocabulary words in the context of the story and discuss their meanings.
- Complete a vocabulary activity (page 9).
- Grow a vegetable garden (page 11).
- Decode the Creighton dialect (page 12).
- Study the history of Fort Sumter and the beginning of the Civil War (page 13).
- Begin "Reader's Response Journals" (page 14).
- Administer the Section 1 quiz (page 10).
- Introduce the vocabulary list for Section 2 (page 8).

Lesson 3
- Read chapters 4 and 5. As you read, note the vocabulary words in the context of the story and discuss their meanings.
- Complete a vocabulary activity (page 9).
- Let the students design their own living annex (page 16).
- Have small groups learn about and report on significant people of the Civil War (page 17).
- Complete a map relating to significant Civil War locations (page 18).
- Create current day political cartoons (page 19).
- Administer the Section 2 quiz (page 15).
- Introduce the vocabulary list for Section 3 (page 8).

Lesson 4
- Read chapters 6 and 7. As you read, note the vocabulary words in the context of the story and discuss their meanings.
- Complete a vocabulary activity (page 9).
- Make a Civil War-era food: cornbread (page 21).
- Develop a plan for making a difference in the classroom or school, and implement it (page 22).
- Write friendly letters filled with news (page 23).
- Complete and discuss the "Growing Up" worksheet (page 24).
- Administer the Section 3 quiz (page 20).
- Introduce the vocabulary list for Section 4 (page 8).

Lesson 5
- Read chapters 8 and 9. As you read, note the vocabulary words in the context of the story and discuss their meanings.
- Complete a vocabulary activity (page 9).
- Complete the "Nourishment" activity which concerns food sources and survival (page 26).
- Construct model barns (page 27).
- Figure area and volume for the Creighton's barn (page 28).
- Write and discuss definitions and examples of respect (page 29).
- Administer the Section 4 quiz (page 25).
- Introduce the vocabulary list for Section 5 (page 8).

Lesson 6
- Read chapters 10–12. As you read, note the vocabulary words in the context of the story and discuss their meanings.
- Complete a vocabulary activity (page 9).
- Create dioramas for one of the "Three Important Events" (page 31).
- Hold classroom debates on several war outcomes (page 32).
- Learn about and compare the casualties of the war (page 33).
- Consider what would happen if war broke out in the students' home town (page 34).
- Administer the Section 5 quiz (page 30).

Lesson 7
- Discuss any questions your students may have about the story (page 35).
- Assign book reports and research projects (pages 36 and 37).
- Begin work on the culminating activity (pages 38–41).

Lesson 8
- Administer unit tests 1, 2, and/or 3 (pages 42–44).
- Discuss the test answers and responses.
- Discuss the students' opinions and enjoyment of the book.
- Provide a list of related reading (page 45) for the students, or provide the books themselves.

Lesson 9
- Prepare and host a Civil War Exhibition (pages 38–41).

4

About the Author

Irene Hunt was born on May 18, 1907, in Newton, Illinois, to Franklin and Sarah Land Hunt. At the age of seven, her life took a dramatic turn when her father died. She would later describe the experience of the death of a parent in her Newbery Award-winning novel, *Up a Road Slowly*.

Miss Hunt is an intelligent and educated woman who earned a Master of Arts degree from the University of Minnesota in 1946. This was, of course, in a time when few women attended college at all, let alone earned an advanced degree. After being a public school teacher for 15 years, Hunt went on to teach at the University of South Dakota from 1946 to 1950. She then returned to the Illinois public schools and eventually became a consultant in language arts.

Miss Hunt's first novel, *Across Five Aprils*, was published in 1964. It was the sole runner-up for the Newbery Medal in 1965. It also received the Charles W. Follett Award in 1964 and the American Notable Book Award in 1965. She followed the novel with *Up a Road Slowly*, the story of a seven-year-old girl whose mother slowly dies. The story follows the girl over a 10-year period of time, and critics believe that Hunt's own feelings and experiences of her father's death are depicted in the work of fiction. *Up a Road Slowly* won the Newbery Medal in 1967. Other novels followed, including *Lottery Rose*, *Trail of Apple Blossoms*, and *No Promises in the Wind*.

Of *Across Five Aprils*, Hunt has said, "I didn't plan my first book for a certain age group. I don't want to aim at a special age of reader. I write when I have something to say, and I hope to say it as well and as gracefully as I can." Undoubtedly, thousands of readers of all ages have agreed over the last few decades that her classic novel is beautifully and engagingly written.

Hunt has also commented on the particular qualifications needed by an author of worthwhile fiction for children and young adults. She says that the writer must have ". . . a close affinity with his own childhood . . . He must remember the anxieties and uncertainties . . . his reactions to tastes, to smells, to colors . . . his love of a kind hand, his fear of a harsh mouth." The reader finds all these memories within Hunt's novels, and certainly that is a reason why they remain well-received to this day.

On awarding her the Newbery Medal, the Newbery-Caldecott committee said that Hunt's work, ". . . concerns itself with the timeless problems of all young people groping for independence and maturity." This is, in fact, the primary thrust of her fiction, and therefore her works are ideally suited to adolescents and young adults. Certainly, Miss Hunt's work will be "remembered."

Across Five Aprils

by Irene Hunt

(Berkley Books, 1964)

(available in CAN, UK, & AUS from Penguin Putnam)

Across Five Aprils is the coming-of-age story of a boy whose adolescence is marked by the advent, activities, and outcome of the American Civil War. Born the youngest of 12 children to an Illinois farm family, Jethro Creighton is nine years old in April of 1861, when military forces of the Southern states fire on Union forces at Fort Sumter. This was the first event of the four-year war, and Jethro's life and family would never be the same.

The Creighton family is a close-knit one, but the war divides the home just as it does the union of states. Jethro's most-beloved brother, Bill, sympathizes with the plight of the Southern farmer and chooses to fight on the rebel side. Other brothers, a cousin, and Shadrach Yale, Jethro's hero and his sister's sweetheart, fight for the North. Jethro loves them all but is distraught by the split, as well as the loss of those who are dear to him.

At the age of nine, Jethro shares all the farm work with his father, work that was formerly done with the help of five older boys and men. Taking on adult responsibilities and adult concerns, Jethro is forced to grow up quickly, losing much of his childhood to work and worry.

Before the outbreak of war, the adults' talk of tension among the states is of little concern to Jethro. However, as the war progresses, Jethro becomes an expert on battles and politics, even writing a personal letter to President Abraham Lincoln and receiving a treasured reply. Jethro also takes the opportunity during the years of the war to advance his education, teaching himself geography, grammar, and other subjects to improve his mind and abilities.

When Jethro's brother, Tom, is killed in the war, the family is devastated by the loss as well as the suspicion that the bullet Tom received might have come from his brother Bill's gun. Months later, while in a prisoner-of-war camp, Bill is able to send his family word that he was not involved in the battle where Tom died. This information is a small but welcome comfort to the family.

The final blow comes with the news that rocks the entire nation. Abraham Lincoln, the president who fought tirelessly throughout the war for resolution and peace, is shot and killed by an assassin's bullet. Jethro and millions of others feel as though the loss of the president is too much to bear. For many, he seemed the only hope for reconciliation among the states.

Gratefully, along with all the tragedies, there are blessings and triumphs for Jethro and his family. Jethro's cousin, Eb, who had become a deserter, is able to return honorably to his post, and Shadrach returns home healthy and strong, despite nearly dying in battle. Jethro also learns that he will be allowed to go with his sister and her new husband to Pennsylvania to earn an advanced education, a dream he had barely allowed himself to dream.

The novel carefully and powerfully depicts the inner thoughts and struggles of a boy who must cope with extraordinary obstacles during one of the most difficult and impressionable times of life. With the help of his loving family and his own good instincts, Jethro comes through the experience as a strong, honorable, and commendable young man.

6

Before the Book

Here are some activities that may work well to help your students focus on the literature.

- Before you begin reading *Across Five Aprils*, help the students to develop a feel for the historical and cultural framework in which the book is set.
- Predict what the story may be about based on the title and cover illustration.
- Consider when the book was copyrighted. Discuss what might be significant about that time in history as compared to the events of the book.
- Ask the class to read and discuss the Author's Note at the back of the book. What does this tell about Irene Hunt's motives for writing the novel?
- Discuss other books by Irene Hunt about which students may have heard or read.
- Discuss the genre of historical fiction.
- Write brief, fictionalized accounts of significant events in your country's history.
- Discuss the American Civil War, providing facts concerning length of time, locations, casualties, causes of death, affects on the average citizenry, and so forth.
- Discuss internal wars fought throughout time and throughout the world. Compare effects and outcomes of these wars.
- Read first-hand accounts of the Civil War from published letters and diaries.
- Ask the students if they have any family stories, letters, or artifacts passed down from the time of the Civil War.
- Divide the class into two teams. Have one team research the South's reasons for leaving the Union in 1861 and have the other research the North's reasons for fighting the Civil War. Let the students debate whether the North and South could have avoided going to war, considering their feelings on these issues.
- Let the students know that during the Civil War, boys as young as they are joined the Union and Confederate armies. Ask them to discuss whether that would be possible today. Also discuss the changing role of women in the military.
- Answer the following questions either in class discussion or in writing.
  - —Is there any cause for which you would willingly fight in a war?
  - —How would you feel if the work of five people was suddenly given to you to complete? Would you do it?
  - —What would you do if you had to make a decision, but all available options would be difficult and dangerous?
  - —Which president or national leader do you most admire and why?
  - —What makes a person a hero?
  - —What do you think it means to be educated?
- Write descriptions of what makes a person strong. Allow students to determine whether strength is physical, emotional, psychological, spiritual, or a combination of any of these.
- Set up a time line bulletin board to be used while reading the book to mark significant events that take place in the war and in the Creighton family.
- Post a large blank map of the eastern United States. Have students research each location mentioned in the book and mark it on the map.

Vocabulary Lists

On this page are vocabulary lists which correspond to each sectional grouping of chapters, as outlined in the table of contents. Vocabulary activity ideas can be found on page 9.

SECTION 1
Chapters 1–3

acrid	comeuppance	feint	militia	pious	tremulous
aloofness	compelling	folly	nullification	prestige	tumult
arrogant	Confederate	furrow	oratory	prim	typhoid fever
blithely	desolate	imminence	passive	reverberations	unyielding
buoyancy	dissipate	industrialists	paternal	Scriptures	wiry
burlap	elicited	inflamed	perry	secession	
Calvinism	emancipator	loam	physics	sullen	

SECTION 2
Chapters 4–5

abolitionist	belligerently	diluted	inevitably	prospect	tyrannical
admonitions	chafing	dispel	keener	reluctant	unconditional
allusion	coarse	fare	livery	scornful	vigor
annex	commenced	forbidding	paisley	skepticism	wanly
appalled	constriction	forte	pallor	soberly	
astute	curt	inconspicuous	plaintive	sympathizers	
attainments	detaining	indistinct	pompous	tethered	

SECTION 3
Chapters 6–7

amended	chagrin	frailty	integrity	prophecy	sundry
anguish	culprit	gullibility	malice	quagmire	switches (noun)
baubles	demoted	hoax	mean	raucous	tenacious
bolstering	dismayed	immunity	niche	reinforcements	tranquil
canopy	enfeebled	implements	ominous	ruffians	zeal
casing	entrenchments	imposed	plaudits	ruthlessly	
casualty	flourish	inept	prestige	spite	

SECTION 4
Chapters 8–9

ancestral	contagion	faltering	haunch	mannerism	ridicule
antagonized	Copperheads	forestall	hindsight	provoke	sheepishly
audible	credence	futile	impudent	registrars	staunch
baptismal	demoralized	gangrenous	interminable	reiterated	tenacity
blusterer	dense	genially	interspersed	remorse	travail
boasting	desertion	ghastly	lank	retreat	vex
compatriots	draft	grimace	magnitude	revile	

SECTION 5
Chapters 10–12

amnesty	conspiracy	egotism	inept	pawns	tenacity
arrogant	cynically	enlivened	invective	plundering	throes
assuaged	deluded	faring	mired	presumption	verified
bigots	desolation	folly	obscurity	provender	vindictiveness
brooked	detachments	fortification	onslaught	relegated	
clemency	detractors	humility	paeans	speculations	
clench	discredited	imminence	pandemonium	taut	

Vocabulary Activity Ideas

Help students learn and retain the vocabulary words in *Across Five Aprils* by providing interesting vocabulary activities. Here are some engaging ideas to try:

☐ Have students create their own **crossword** or **word search puzzles**, using vocabulary words from the novel.

☐ Challenge the students to a **vocabulary bee**. This is similar to a spelling bee, but in addition to spelling each word correctly, the game participants must correctly define the words.

☐ Play **Vocabulary Concentration**. The goal of this game is to match vocabulary words with their definitions. Divide the class into groups of 2–5 students. Have the students make two sets of cards in the same size and color. On one set have them write the vocabulary words. On the second set have them write the definitions. All cards are mixed together and placed facedown on a table. A player picks two cards. If the pair matches the word with its definition, the player keeps the cards and takes another turn. If the cards do not match, they are returned to their places facedown on the table and another player takes a turn. Players must concentrate to remember the locations of words and definitions. The game continues until all matches have been made. This is an ideal activity for free exploration time.

☐ Have the students practice their writing skills by composing sentences and paragraphs in which multiple vocabulary words are used correctly. Ask them to share their **compact vocabulary** sentences and paragraphs with the class.

☐ Ask the students to write paragraphs which use the vocabulary words to present **history lessons** relating to the historic events of the book.

☐ Challenge the students to use a specific vocabulary word from the story at least **10 times in one day**. They must keep a record of when, how, and why the word was used.

☐ As a group activity, instruct the students to work together to create an **illustrated dictionary** of the vocabulary words. They can add other vocabulary from the book, as desired.

☐ **Play Twenty Clues** with the entire class. In this game, one student selects a vocabulary word and gives clues about it, one by one, until someone in the class can guess the word.

☐ Play **Vocabulary Charades**. In this game, vocabulary words are enacted while others try to guess.

Quiz Time

1. Describe Jethro—what kind of boy he is and what he looks like.

    _____

    _____

    _____

2. Where does this story take place?

    _____

3. Choose three important, fictional characters (besides Jethro) who are introduced in this section and write a few words to describe each.

    _____

    _____

    _____

4. Why does Eb live with the Creightons?

    _____

    _____

5. What is the relationship between Bill and John?

    _____

    _____

6. What is the relationship between Jenny and Shadrach Yale?

    _____

    _____

7. How does cousin Wilse Graham attempt to justify the fact that he keeps slaves?

    _____

    _____

8. What news does Shad bring from town?

    _____

    _____

9. How do Jethro's feelings about war change from chapter one to chapter three?

    _____

    _____

10. Why does Bill choose to fight with the Confederates?

    _____

    _____

Vegetable Garden

Jethro and his family live off the land. They work hard through the seasons to grow a bountiful harvest. Although it is unlikely you have the means or opportunity to grow a crop on the scale the Creightons do, you can certainly share in the experience by planting and growing a small vegetable garden. The entire class can be involved in the preparation and care of the garden, and the fruits of your labor can be enjoyed in a class party at harvest time.

To begin, do the following:

- Have the class research to determine which vegetables will grow best in your area.

- Find a small area of land at your school where your garden can be planted and tended. If no land is available, use large pots or window boxes with good drainage. These will need to be brought out into the sun daily.

- Make a schedule of responsibilities for each student so that everyone has an opportunity to tend the garden and all the needs of the garden are met every day. (Your garden should be fine if unattended over the weekends.)

- Ask for donations from parents or local nurseries and home merchandise stores for the supplies you will need (e.g., seeds, soil, fertilizer, mulch, watering cans, spades, hoes, etc.).

- Once you have decided on your garden's contents and location and have gathered your materials, work as a class to plant your garden.

Here are some steps to follow:

1. Dig up the soil about 12" (30 cm). Break it up and mix it with fertilizer.

2. Rake the soil smooth before planting.

3. Plant the seeds according to the package directions.

4. Spread mulch over the planted soil to help prevent weeds and to keep the soil moist.

5. Place small signs in the soil near each type of seed so you will remember what was planted there.

6. When the plant grows, pinch off a small portion at the top of the main stem to make the plant grow fuller and more productive.

7. In order to provide each plant ample room to grow, pull up and replant any plants growing too closely together.

8. Remember to water and weed regularly.

Understanding Dialects

The author of *Across Five Aprils* gives the reader a clear understanding of how the Creightons speak by the way in which she writes the dialogue. If the reader pays careful attention, he or she can almost hear the dialect of the family.

A dialect is a special way of speaking that is particular to a group of people in a certain area. The Creighton dialect is a combination of the midwest and southern United States dialects of the mid-1800s. It is easy to understand once the reader becomes a little familiar with it.

I. In small groups, translate the lines of dialogue below into standard English.

1. "Yore hopes is makin' a fool of yore reason, Jeth."

_____

2. "It 'mazes me, Jeth, it does fer a fact, the way you kin recollect all the things Shad tells you and how you kin put them from his way of talkin' into mine."

_____

3. "Be you spent, Jethro?"

_____

4. "I've got a crock of lettuce fer you, Jeth, though I'm terr'ble wasteful in pickin' it too young."

_____

5. "Much as I keer fer my fam'ly, a crowded cabin chafes me; it allus has."

_____

II. Work as a team to rewrite each of the following lines into the dialect spoken by the Creighton family.

1. How are you today, Jethro?

_____

2. I am going to work on the potato crop.

_____

3. Jethro is the youngest of Mr. and Mrs. Creighton's 12 children.

_____

4. My family has many different feelings about the possibility of war.

_____

5. When will I see you again, Bill?

_____

Fort Sumter

The following events led to the beginning of the American Civil War. Use reference books to help you arrange the events in order. Write them in the correct numbered spaces.

a. Major Robert Anderson moves his garrison to Fort Sumter in the Charleston Harbor.

b. Six more states secede, and Lincoln takes office. Fort Sumter remains one of two Southern forts under Union control.

c. South Carolina passes an order of secession.

d. Governor Francis Pickens demands that the Union surrender Fort Sumter.

e. The United States declares war on the Confederacy.

f. The Confederates at Fort Johnson fire on the Union soldiers in Fort Sumter.

g. Major Anderson surrenders.

h. Abraham Lincoln wins the presidential election of 1860.

i. *The Star of the West*, a Union ship, attempts to deliver reinforcements and supplies to Fort Sumter. It is fired upon and leaves.

j. Lincoln orders an attempt for provisions to be sent to Fort Sumter, where soldiers are in danger of starvation.

k. All Northern and Southern negotiations cease.

1. _____

2. _____

3. _____

4. _____

5. _____

6. _____

7. _____

8. _____

9. _____

10. _____

11. _____

Reader's Response Journals

One reason avid readers are drawn to literature is what it does for them on a personal level. They are intrigued with how it triggers their imaginations, what it makes them ponder, and how it makes them see and shape themselves. To aid your students in experiencing this for themselves, incorporate Reader's Response Journals into your plans. In these journals, students can be encouraged to respond to the story in a number of ways. Here are a few ideas.

☐ Tell the students that the purpose of the journal is to record their thoughts, ideas, observations, and questions as they read the book.

☐ Provide students with, or ask them to suggest, topics or prompts from the story that may stimulate writing. Here are two examples from the chapters in Section 1.

    —Jethro feels excited at the thought of war until it becomes a reality. Have you ever changed your mind about something once it became real for you?

    —Bill and John find themselves on opposite sides concerning the war. Have you ever had a significant disagreement with someone to whom you are very close?

☐ After reading each chapter, students can write one or more new thing they have learned.

☐ Ask the students to draw their responses to certain events or characters in the story.

☐ Suggest to your students that they write diary-type responses to their reading by selecting a character and describing events from the character's point of view.

☐ Encourage the students to bring their journal ideas to life by using them to create plays, stories, songs, art displays, and debates.

☐ Allow students time to write in their journals daily. To evaluate the journals, you may wish to use the following guidelines.

    • Read students' personal reflections, but make no corrections and assign no letter grade for content or craft. Give credit for effort, or assign a grade according to the number of entries made.

    • Non-judgmental responses should be made as you read the journals in order to let the students know you are reading and enjoying their responses. Types of appropriate responses include the following:

    —"You have really found what is important in the story."

    —"You have made me feel as if I am there."

    —"If you feel comfortable, I would like you to share this with the class. I think they will enjoy it as much as I have."

Quiz Time

1. At the beginning of this section, what has Ulysses S. Grant done to make many Northerners believe the war might soon end?

   _____

   _____

2. What does Tom mean when he writes, "You tell Jeth that bein' a soljer aint so much"?

   _____

   _____

3. What does Ellen allow Jethro to do after they receive Tom's letter?

   _____

   _____

4. Why is Ellen ashamed of herself concerning coffee?

   _____

   _____

5. Who does Jethro meet on the way to Newton, and what does he want Jethro to do?

   _____

   _____

6. What gift does Sam Gardiner give to Jethro?

   _____

   _____

7. Who is Ross Milton, and what does he do for Jethro?

   _____

   _____

8. At the town store, what does Jethro say in defense of Bill?

   _____

   _____

9. What does Dave Burdow do for Jethro?

   _____

   _____

10. Why do you think Dave might have done this?

   _____

   _____

Extra Credit: On your own, do some research to find the source and meaning of "Thou too, Brutus," as well as Shad's meaning when he says it. To earn extra credit, this assignment is due

_____ .

My Annex

Shadrach Yale is the local school teacher. Customarily, the school teacher of a small town boards with the students' families; however, Shad objects, claiming that every man needs his own space. The board agrees, and an annex is added to the school house. Shad furnishes and decorates it to suit his own ways and personality. In rich and inviting detail, the author tells the reader what Shad has done.

Imagine you become the school teacher when Shad moves away. Below is an outline of your annex from above. Design your room and its furnishings as though you are looking down on them. On the back of this paper, write a detailed paragraph explaining how you decorated your annex.

Fireplace

Extension: Build a three-dimensional model of your annex.

Important People of the Civil War

Here is a list of historical figures who were prominent during the time of the Civil War. Many of these names are mentioned in *Across Five Aprils*. Others in this list, although not mentioned in the book, were also influential at the time for various reasons.

In small groups, choose one figure to research. Answer the questions at the bottom of the page, regarding the chosen individual. Follow the report directions to prepare a presentation you will make to the class.

People

As a group, choose one individual from the list below:

- Clara Barton
- John Brown
- James Buchanan
- Jefferson Davis
- Frederick Douglass
- Ulysses S. Grant
- Stonewall Jackson
- Robert E. Lee
- Abraham Lincoln
- George B. McClellan
- Dred Scott
- William T. Sherman
- Harriet Tubman

Jefferson Davis

Abraham Lincoln

Questions

Research to find answers to these questions for the person you have chosen.

1. Who is this person?
2. What are the significant events of this person's life?
3. Why is this person important in regards to the Civil War?

Report

Prepare a report about the person, following these steps.

1. Draw an illustration of the person on standard-size drawing paper.
2. Attach the picture to the center of a poster board.
3. At the top of the board, write the person's name.
4. Below his or her name, write the person's significance to the Civil War.
5. Around the picture, write the significant events of the person's life.
6. Choose a spokesperson from your group. When the time comes to make the report to the class, the spokesperson will tell the class the information you found. Others in the group can hold the display for the class to see.

Map It Out

Here is an outline map of the southeastern United States in 1862. In chapter four, Shad draws a map of this area for Jethro. He adds Confederate/Union designations, significant rivers, and Forts Donelson and Henry in order to show Jethro the importance of the fort victories as well as the work still ahead for the Union soldiers.

Using the map below, do the following.

1. Label the states.

2. Mark a **C** in all Confederate states after the victories at Donelson and Henry.

3. Mark a **U** in all Union states after the victories at Donelson and Henry.

4. Draw and label the Mississippi River, the Tennessee River, the Ohio River, and the Cumberland River.

5. Mark a dot on the map for Fort Donelson.

6. Mark a star (☆) on the map for Fort Henry.

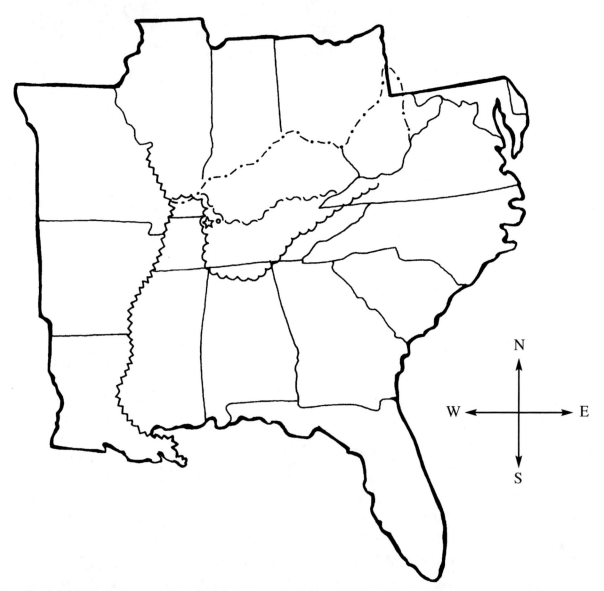

Discussion: By looking at your map and taking into account what Shad said, what is the significance of the Forts Donelson and Henry victories?

Political Cartoons

During the Civil War, the art of political cartoons in newspapers grew in frequency and significance. Political cartoonists throughout the country used cartoons to convey their thoughts and feelings concerning the war and its leaders. In chapter five of *Across Five Aprils*, the author describes a cartoon that Jethro sees in Ross Milton's office. It shows Abraham Lincoln demoting an incompetent General McClellan. The cartoon would look something like this:

Take a look in your local newspaper. You are sure to find one or more political cartoons done in a similar manner. Generally there are few words in such cartoons; the picture tells most of the story.

What are some things happening in the world of politics today? Choose a topic, and on a separate sheet of paper, draw a political cartoon of your own. Be sure the message is clear, and be prepared to share your cartoon with the class.

Teacher Note: Discuss the meaning of the cartoon Jethro sees.

Quiz Time

1. What happens in chapter six that puts an end to Jethro's childhood?

   _____

   _____

2. What does Jenny receive, and why does it anger Jethro?

   _____

   _____

3. What does Nancy do to help Jethro?

   _____

   _____

4. What do "ruffians" throw down at the Creighton's gate to warn them of future punishment?

   _____

   _____

5. What is the future punishment?

   _____

   _____

6. What news does Dan Lawrence bring to the Creightons?

   _____

   _____

7. For whom was Jethro named?

   _____

   _____

8. Where do the Creighton's record their births, deaths, and marriages?

   _____

   _____

9. Where are the three oldest Creighton children?

   _____

   _____

   _____

10. How does Sam Gardiner get vengeance on Guy Wortman?

   _____

   _____

   _____

Civil War Cornbread

Jenny calls herself one of the best cooks around. Here is a recipe from the time of the Civil War that is still very popular in the United States today. Try it on your own or as a class. Enjoy it during your culminating activities or as a special treat any time.

Ingredients:

- 1 cup (250 mL) yellow cornmeal
- 1 cup (250 mL) all-purpose flour
- 2 tablespoons (30 mL) sugar
- 4 teaspoons (20 mL) baking powder
- $\frac{1}{2}$ teaspoon (2.5 mL) salt
- 1 cup (250 mL) milk
- $\frac{1}{4}$ cup (65 mL) shortening
- 1 egg

Materials:

- mixing bowl
- wooden spoon
- measuring cups and spoons
- 8" x 8" x 2" (20 cm x 20 cm x 5 cm) pan
- oven
- oven mitts

Preparation:

1. Heat the oven to 425° F (220° C).
2. Blend all ingredients, and then beat vigorously by hand for about one minute.
3. Grease the pan with shortening.
4. Pour the mixture into the pan.
5. Bake until golden brown (about 20–25 minutes).

Helping Hands

When Matt Creighton falls ill and becomes the victim of Guy Wortman and his gang, scores of neighbors and friends come from miles around to help. They work his farm, guard his house, give him a new watchdog, replace his lost farm equipment, and much more. The people prove that helping hands can make a tremendous difference.

In small groups or as a class, you will determine a way to be "helping hands" in your own classroom or school. Follow these two simple steps:

1. Choose a classroom or school need where you can make a difference.

2. Work together to make it happen!

It really is that simple once you put your mind to it. A little effort goes a long way.

Here are some things to keep in mind when making your group plans.

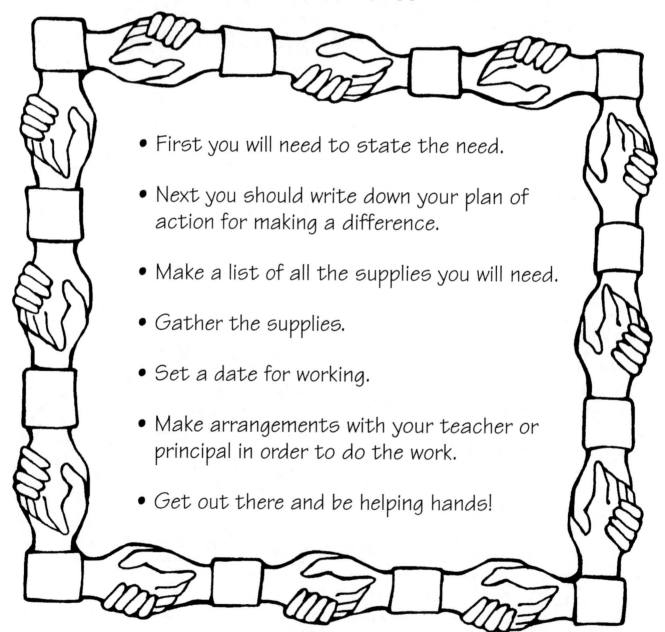

- First you will need to state the need.

- Next you should write down your plan of action for making a difference.

- Make a list of all the supplies you will need.

- Gather the supplies.

- Set a date for working.

- Make arrangements with your teacher or principal in order to do the work.

- Get out there and be helping hands!

What's New, Friend?

Whenever the Creighton family receives a letter, the entire family joins in hearing the news. Letters from family and friends become especially important during the time of war. Today, people use telephones and even computers to communicate with one another, but letter writing is still a valuable option.

Think about all the things happening in your life right now. Using the friendly letter format on this page, write a letter to a friend or family member, telling him or her the latest news about you. Write your letter on a separate sheet of paper. After your teacher reads it, you can mail the letter. The best part is, you might get a letter in return!

_____
your street address

_____
your city, state, and zip code

_____
today's date

Dear _____,
    name of person

_____

_____

_____

_____

_____

_____

_____
all your news

_____
closing (Your friend, Sincerely, Best wishes, etc.)

_____
your name

Growing Up

From the time the Civil War begins, Jethro grows up quickly, particularly when his father becomes ill. He misses many normal experiences of his childhood and adolescence, since he must take on adult responsibilities at an early age. However, he does experience some significant milestones of growing up, such as the responsibility to shop for the family, driving the family wagon, and being in charge of the family's farm.

Regardless of the details of your own life, you have experienced many milestones along the way, markers along your path of growing up. When you were around one year of age, you probably began to walk. When you started school, you could probably write your name and tie your shoes. These were all things that showed you were growing up.

In the spaces below, make a list of several important milestones for you, such as being allowed to stay home alone, ordering your own food at a restaurant, spending the night away from home, or anything else you can think of. Write the milestones in the left column and your approximate age when you first did them in the right. Then answer the question at the bottom of the page.

Milestones	Age

Answer: What will it take for you to be really grown up?

_____

_____

_____

_____

Quiz Time

1. What does Dave Burdow send to Jethro?

_____

_____

2. What does Shad write is missing in General McClellan?

_____

_____

3. By the winter of 1862, what had thousands of young soldiers begun to do? Why?

_____

_____

4. What is Point Prospect and why is it dangerous?

_____

_____

5. How does a man avoid the draft during the Civil War?

_____

_____

6. What happens to Hig Phillips?

_____

_____

7. Why do the Federal Registrars come to the Creighton home?

_____

_____

_____

8. What does Jethro discover in the woods around John and Nancy's farm?

_____

_____

9. What does Jethro do to help Eb?

_____

_____

_____

10. What is the main idea of Lincoln's letter to Jethro?

_____

_____

Nourishment

Most of us get plenty of food to eat each day. We seldom think about what it would be like not to have enough or any food. We can just open the cupboard or go to the store, and there it is. In *Across Five Aprils,* Eb is alone and in danger of starving. He is very lucky to find any food at all.

A. In the chart below, make a list of everything you eat in one day and where you got the food (for example, the refrigerator, your mother, a restaurant, etc.).

Food	Source

B. Look around your backyard, the schoolyard, or a local park and try to find things you could eat if you had to. Make a list of those things on the back of this paper. Be prepared to come to class to discuss what you found. You will also discuss the class's ability to survive as compared to Eb's.

Barn Raising

Neighbors come from miles around to help the Creightons construct a new barn. Working together, the group is able to replace the old barn in just one day's time.

Gatherings such as this to build a barn for a neighbor are called barn raisings. Nobody charges a fee for the work. Everyone just pitches in willingly, with the expectation that if he or she is ever in need, the neighbors will be there to help him or her as well.

Now it is your turn to have a "barn" raising of your own. Gather into small groups and work together to construct a small-scale model of a barn.

Materials:

- ruler
- building materials (such as craft sticks, cardboard, or clay)
- adhesive materials (such as craft glue or string)
- baseboard (such as sturdy cardboard or a thin sheet of wood)
- scissors, paint, and paintbrushes, as needed
- paper and pencil

Directions:

1. Work together to plan a design for your barn. Draw it on paper, figuring the dimensions (height, width, and length).
2. Make a list of the specific materials you will need.
3. Gather your materials.
4. Divide up the work plan so that each of you are responsible for a part of the finished barn.
5. Construct your individual pieces and attach them, completing your model barn on the baseboard.
6. If desired, decorate the baseboard with painted grass, trees, and other plants.
7. Present your finished barn to the class, telling them about your design and how you worked together to complete it. (For example, who did what, and how well did you work together?)

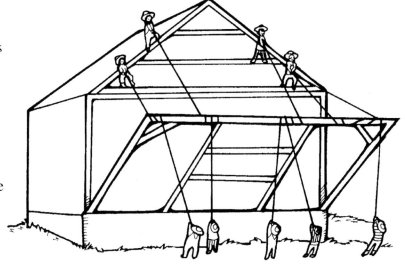

Class Discussion:

Imagine that you had done this project on your own. Discuss the differences in time and the finished product, comparing the group's work with what your own might have been.

How Big Should We Make It?

Before the Creighton's new barn could be built, someone had to measure logs to construct the barn with the proper dimensions. The floor size of the barn would have been determined by finding its *area*. Area is measured with this formula:

area = width x length (a = w x l)

To determine the overall size of the barn, volume would need to be measured. Volume is measured with this formula:

volume = width x height x length (v = w x h x l)

Use the formulas above to answer the following problems. (The problems are done in standard measurement since that is the form the Creightons would have used. Metric measurements are given as well.) Area is written in square feet; volume is written in cubic feet.

1. The Creightons want the width of the barn to be 20 feet (6 meters) and the length to be 30 feet (9 meters). What is the area?

   _____

2. To the above measurements, the Creightons are adding a height of 10 feet (3 meters). What is the volume?

   _____

3. The family decides that the width of their barn should be 22 feet (7 meters) and the length 28 feet (8.5 meters). What area will they have?

   _____

4. To the measurements in number three, the family want to add a height of 16 feet (5 meters). What volume will they have?

   _____

5. The Creightons want a barn with an area of 375 square feet (34 sq. meters) and a length of 25 feet (8 meters). What width do they need?

   _____

6. The family would like a barn with a volume of 3600 cubic feet (108 cubic meters). They know they want a length of 20 feet (6 meters) and a height of 10 feet (3 meters). What width do they need?

   _____

Respect

Respect is very important to Jethro. He wants to be respected for the work he does as well as the way he presents himself, particularly in his speech. It is also important to him that he shows respect to others who deserve it. When he writes to President Lincoln, he takes careful pains to do so respectfully.

Answer each of the questions below. Think carefully about each one before answering, and provide detailed, thorough answers. Afterwards, you and your class will discuss everybody's answers and opinions—showing respect to one another when you do!

1. What does respect mean to you?

_____

_____

_____

_____

2. To whom in your life do you show respect? Make a list, and give reasons why you show respect to each person.

_____

_____

_____

_____

_____

_____

4. How do you show respect to others?

_____

_____

_____

_____

5. How would you like others to show respect to you?

_____

_____

_____

_____

Quiz Time

1. At the Battle of Gettysburg, what happens to Shad?

   _____

   _____

2. What does Jenny do on August 14, 1863?

   _____

   _____

3. What does President Lincoln offer in his proclamation of amnesty?

   _____

   _____

   _____

4. What does Shad send to Jethro that are "like gifts to the lonely boy"?

   _____

   _____

5. What happens of significance when John is caring for rebel prisoners?

   _____

   _____

   _____

6. What news does Bill send to his parents?

   _____

   _____

   _____

7. What is Ed Turner afraid of in regards to the burning and looting of Southern towns by Union soldiers?

   _____

   _____

8. What troubles does Ross Milton see for the freed black people?

   _____

   _____

   _____

9. What news devastates Jethro after April 14, 1864?

   _____

10. What does Shad promise to do for Jethro when he goes to college?

    _____

    _____

Three Important Events

There were numerous important events throughout the Civil War, and *Across Five Aprils* relates many of them. The final chapters of the book mention three in particular, and these three are of special significance. The first takes place at Gettysburg, where President Lincoln makes his memorable **Gettysburg Address** on November 19, 1863. The second occurs at **Appomattox Court House** on April 9, 1864, and the third at **Ford's Theater** on April 14, 1864. They all have important meaning for Jethro.

The Gettysburg Address, although short and simple, struck a chord with the American people that still reverberates today. It was particularly poignant in that it followed one of the bloodiest battles of the entire war. Jethro is aware of all the discussion surrounding the address, and he and his mother believe "It has the ring of the Scriptures about it."

Appomattox Court House is the scene of the peace that ends the Civil War. It was there that General Robert E. Lee officially surrendered his army to General Ulysses S. Grant. The Union has won the war, and everywhere Jethro looks, people are celebrating. However, those close to Jethro remind him that the win is not a "perfect pearl."

Ford's Theater is the scene of one of the most devastating casualties of the war, the assassination of President Lincoln by the southerner, John Wilkes Booth. Jethro and all his family are heartsick at this news. Booth had originally intended to kidnap the President, but when the Southern capital of Richmond, Virginia, fell, Booth decided instead to kill him. His plan was unfortunately successful, although he himself was found and killed less than two weeks later.

Activity:

Choose any of the three scenes described above. Do some research to find more details about the event. Then create a diorama*, depicting the scene you have chosen. Be neat and detailed, doing your best work. Be sure to adhere to historical fact in your presentation.

*A diorama is a three-dimensional depiction of a scene from history or a work of fiction. The scene is created in layers (or rows) of images within a box. A hole is cut in one end of the box so that an individual can look through the hole to view the scene. The scene should be constructed so that all layers can be seen from the viewing hole.

Debate

A debate is argumentation both for and against a proposition. The proposition is a precise statement worded in the affirmative. It makes clear both the affirmative and negative positions.

You can hold classroom debates to consider some of the actual and conceivable outcomes of the Civil War. Divide the class into small teams. Assign each team the affirmative or negative of one of the following topics.

- Resolved, that a Confederate who pledges loyalty to the Union and follows the new laws regarding slavery shall receive full immunity.

- Resolved, that any Confederate state with 10 percent of the population voting for readmittance to the Union shall be allowed to return with full benefits.

- Resolved, that any Confederate citizen who returns to the Union shall be compensated for the loss of property incurred during the war.

- Resolved, that all Union soldiers will receive special government grants and loans to compensate for time and money lost in the war.

Instruct the student teams to work together to prepare their arguments. They should do the following:

1. Research to find supportive information and data.

2. Organize their arguments logically and clearly.

3. Challenge one another by finding the weak spots in each other's arguments and responding accordingly.

4. Choose a spokesperson.

When it is time to debate, choose a judge or group of judges. The judge(s) will decide whether the proposition passes or fails.

Here is the standard format for a debate. Adapt it to fit your needs.

- The affirmative speaks for 10 minutes. This is called a constructive speech. The negative listens to the arguments.

- The negative speaks for 10 minutes while the affirmative listens.

- The affirmative speaks a second constructive speech for 10 minutes.

- The negative speaks a second constructive speech for 10 minutes.

- The affirmative gives a rebuttal speech of five minutes. A rebuttal is a direct response to the arguments of the other side.

- The negative gives a rebuttal speech of five minutes.

- The affirmative gives a second rebuttal of five minutes.

- The negative gives a second rebuttal of five minutes.

- The judge(s) determines whether the proposition passes or fails.

Civil War Casualties

Tom Creighton would have been just one of thousands of soldiers who died during the Civil War. Of the 2.2 million Union soldiers who fought, 360,000 died, two-thirds from such diseases as typhoid, malaria, measles, dysentery, and even diarrhea. Casualty numbers for the Confederacy are not as accurate as for the Union; however, it is estimated that approximately 250,000 of the 750,000 to 850,000 total Confederate soldiers died, while another 200,000 were wounded. Approximately 280,000 Union soldiers were wounded as well.

Using the above information, answer these questions.

1. What percentage of total Union soldiers were killed or wounded in the war?

2. What percentage of total Confederate soldiers were killed or wounded in the war?

Look at the key below. Use the key to construct a pictograph that shows the Union and Confederate casualties in these major conflicts of the Civil War. When you have finished making your pictograph, complete the activities and questions below the graph.

Civil War Casualties: North and South

Fort Sumter April 12, 1861	
First Battle of Bull Run July 21, 1861	
Antietam September 17, 1862	
Gettysburg July 1–3, 1863	
Cold Harbor June 1–3, 1864	
Siege of Petersburg June 20, 1864 to April 2, 1865	

KEY	Union	= 10,000 casualties = 1,000 casualties
	Confederacy	= 10,000 casualties = 1,000 casualties

3. On the back of this page, arrange the Union battles in order of most casualties to least casualties. Then, do the same for the Confederate battles. Compare the two.

4. In which battles were there more Union casualties than Confederate?

5. In which battles were there more Confederate casualties than Union?

6. In which battles did the casualties for each side exceed 5,000?

In My Own Backyard

One of the most harrowing aspects of the Civil War for most people was that the war was fought in their own towns and villages. This was not a war fought away from their homes in places previously unfamiliar to them. There was no escaping the reality of war, and every day was a fearful one for people in the midst of the fighting.

Imagine that war has broken out in your country and that battles are being fought in various towns and cities near (and in) where you dwell. In the space below, write an account of what you think your life might be like with war in "your own backyard." Think about everything from family life to school to extra-curricular activities to simple survival. What would war in your town mean to you?

If war broke out "in my own backyard" . . .

Any Questions?

After you finished reading *Across Five Aprils*, did you have some questions that were left unanswered? If so, write them here._____

_____

_____

Work in groups or by yourself to prepare possible answers for some or all of the questions you have asked above and those written below. Do your work on a separate sheet of paper. When you have finished, share your ideas with the class.

- How does the family react when John returns? What does Nancy say and do?
- What is life like for Jethro, living with Shad and Jenny away from home? What does he do? How does he feel?
- Does Bill ever return home? If so, what happens?
- Does Jethro ever meet Bill again? If so, what do they say and do?
- Are the Creightons and Burdows friends after the war? How do they behave to one another?
- How is Eb treated by the family and the community when he returns? How does he feel about himself?
- Does Matt recover from his sickness? What is the rest of his life like?
- Does Benjamin, the oldest Creighton son, ever return from California? If so, what happened to him in the years he was gone? If not, why not?
- Will the Creightons and Wilse Graham get along after the war? Are they able to set aside the strong feelings from the war to be family again?
- What career does Jethro choose? Why?
- What stories of the Civil War does Jethro most often tell his children and grandchildren? Why are these stories important to him?

Book Report Ideas

There are many ways to report on a book; after you have read *Across Five Aprils,* choose a method of reporting that appeals to you. It may be an idea of your own or one of the suggestions given below.

The Eyes Have It

Do a visual report by making a model of a scene from the story, drawing or sculpting a likeness of one or more of the characters, or crafting an important symbol from the book.

Time Capsule

Provide future generations with reasons to read *Across Five Aprils.* Inside a time-capsule-shaped design, neatly write your reasons. You may "bury" the capsule after you have shared it with your class.

Come to Life

A size-appropriate group prepares a scene from the story for dramatization, acts it out, and relates the significance of the scene to the entire book. Costumes and props will add to the dramatization!

Into the Future

Predict what might happen if *Across Five Aprils* were to continue. You may write it as a story in narrative form, write it as a dramatic script, or present it in a visual display.

Guess Who or What

This report takes the form of "Twenty Questions." The reporter gives a series of clues in a general-to-specific order about a character, event, or symbol from the story. After each clue, someone may try to guess the character. After all the clues, if the subject cannot be guessed, the reporter supplies the answer.

A Character Comes to Life

Suppose one of the characters from *Across Five Aprils* came to life and walked into your home or classroom. This report gives the character's point of view as he or she sees, hears, feels, and experiences the world in which you live.

Sales Talk

This is an advertisement to "sell" *Across Five Aprils* to one or more specific groups. You decide on the group to target and the sales pitch you will use. Include some kind of graphics in your presentation.

Coming Attraction

Across Five Aprils is about to be made into a movie and you have been chosen to design the promotional poster. Include the title and author of the book, a listing of the main characters and the contemporary actors who will play them, a drawing of a scene from the book, and a paragraph synopsis of the story that will make audiences want to see the movie.

Literary Interview

This report is done in pairs. One student will pretend to be a character in a story by steeping him- or herself completely in the character's persona. The other student will play the role of a radio or TV interviewer, asking questions which will give the audience insight into the character's life.

Dust Jacket Design

Create a dust jacket for the novel by including the title, author, and an important scene, image, or character on the cover; a book summary on the inside flaps; and a teaser (an enticing summation of the plot), as well as a quotable recommendation for the book (such as "The New York Times calls it the 'best historic novel ever!' ") on the back.

Research Ideas

Describe three things that you read in *Across Five Aprils* that you would like to learn more about.

1. _____

2. _____

3. _____

As you read *Across Five Aprils*, you encountered many real locations, people, and events that require some background knowledge to make the reading more meaningful. To increase your understanding of the book, as well as to appreciate Irene Hunt's craft as a writer, research to find out more about some or all of these topics.

- farming in the 1860s
- Illinois
- Emancipation Proclamation
- Thirteenth Amendment
- Robert E. Lee
- Ulysses S. Grant
- Abraham Lincoln
- Fort Sumter
- Appomattox Court House
- surrender of General Johnson to General Sherman
- The Gettysburg Address
- George McClellan
- Stonewall Jackson
- William Tecumseh Sherman
- Clara Barton
- John Wilkes Booth
- Jefferson Davis
- Dred Scott
- Andersonville Prison
- Antietam
- Battle of the Wilderness
- Chattanooga
- Chickamauga
- Cold Harbor
- Fort Donelson
- Fort Henry

- Fredericksburg
- Gettysburg
- Mobile Bay
- Nashville
- Siege of Petersburg
- Richmond
- Savannah
- Seven Days Battles
- Spotsylvania Court House
- Siege of Vicksburg
- secession of states
- Civil War foods
- Civil War music
- slavery in America
- war heroes
- causes of death in the Civil War
- Army of the Potomac
- Atlanta, Georgia
- Bull Run
- Frederick Douglass
- Stephen Douglass
- John Brown
- abolitionists
- Northern industry circa 1860
- Southern farming circa 1860
- Underground Railroad
- Harriet Tubman

Civil War Exhibition

There are many interesting and exciting ways to culminate the reading and study of such a book as *Across Five Aprils*. Perhaps the most beneficial way is to demonstrate to others what has been learned, combining factual experiences of the Civil War with the fictional and fact-based events of the book. Students can demonstrate their knowledge in a classroom exhibition for parents and other classes.

I. The likeliest place to begin preparing for the exhibition is with the Civil War battles and events of significance. To do so, divide the students into small groups and assign each group a portion of the list below. The groups can mark the locations on a map of the United States (page 39). Then, as a class, transfer the small map notations to a large wall map.

- Antietam
- Appomattox Court House
- Atlanta
- Bull Run
- Chancellorsville
- Chattanooga
- Chickamauga
- Cold Harbor
- Fair Oaks
- Fort Donelson
- Fort Henry
- Fort Sumter
- Franklin
- Fredericksburg
- Gettysburg
- Jackson's Valley Campaign
- Kennesaw Mountain
- Mobile Bay
- Nashville
- Perryville
- Richmond
- Savannah
- Seven Days
- Shiloh
- Siege of Petersburg
- Siege of Vicksburg
- Spotsylvania Court House
- Stones River
- Wilderness

II. Display the map and the Important People posters (page 17) made earlier in the unit. Other activities worth displaying include the following:

- class-grown vegetables or the garden itself (page 11)
- social studies maps (page 18)
- barn models (page 27)
- dioramas (page 31)
- pictographs of war casualties (page 33)
- research projects (page 37)

III. Prepare a Civil War presentation, using the map and classroom exhibits. Divide the story of the Civil War into chronological sections, and give each student (or group) a section to prepare, to memorize, and to share with the audience. (Give the students copies of the outline on page 40 to organize their ideas.) On the day of your exhibit, students will tell their visitors the story of the Civil War, using the displays as props and references.

IV. Send invitations to parents, other classes, and/or the faculty and administration. Let the students write the invitations and hand deliver them. An appropriate invitation form is included on page 41. (It will be fun (and educational) to write the invitations with quill pens and ink wells just as Jethro might have done.)

V. When your guests arrive, serve them your homemade cornbread (page 21) and perhaps some apple cider, milk, or water. If desired, try to speak with the farm dialect of the book (page 12).

Civil War Exhibition: U.S. Map

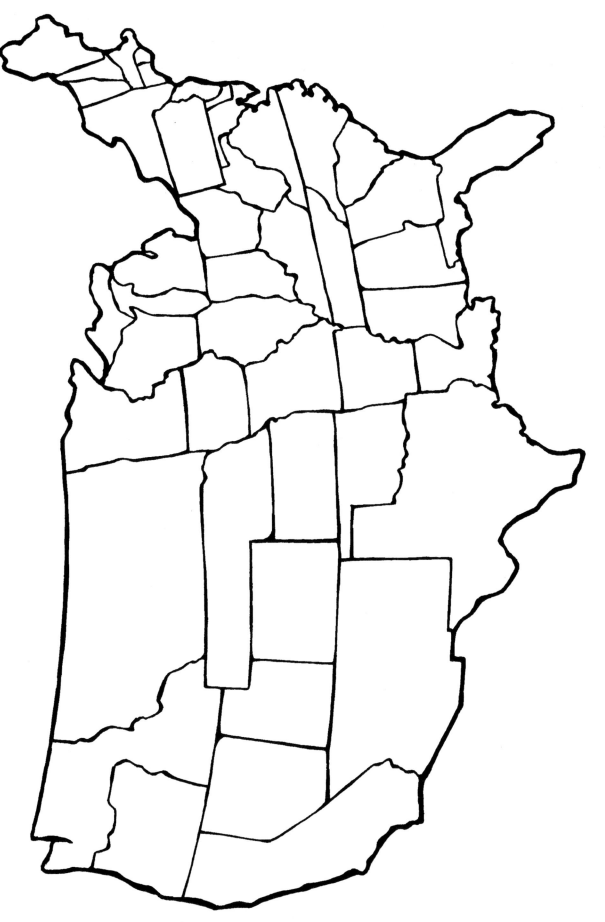

Civil War Exhibition: Presentation Outline

My name is _____.

I will be talking about the period of time from _____ to _____.

The important event(s) during this time is (are) _____

_____

(On the following lines and additional paper, write the rest of your presentation. Give all the necessary details concerning the event(s) of your section of the Civil War. When you have finished writing, practice your presentation so you will be ready at the time of the exhibit.)

_____

_____

_____

_____

_____

_____

_____

_____

_____

_____

_____

_____

_____

_____

_____

_____

_____

_____

_____

_____

_____

_____

Civil War Exhibition: Invitation

Directions: Cut out the invitation along the outside lines. Fold along the dotted line so that the illustration is the cover and it is blank inside. Write the necessary information about the event, the time, and the place inside the invitation.

Objective Test and Essay

Matching:

Match the descriptions of the characters with their names.

1. Jethro Creighton
2. Matt Creighton
3. Ellen Creighton
4. Jenny Creighton
5. Shadrach Yale
6. Dave Burdow
7. Bill Creighton
8. Eb Carron
9. Nancy Creighton
10. Ross Milton
11. Guy Wortman
12. John Creighton
13. Tom Creighton
14. Sam Gardiner

a. teenage girl who falls in love with and marries the schoolteacher
b. young boy who must grow up quickly during the Civil War
c. Union son who fights for the Confederacy
d. newspaper editor and friend to the Creighton family
e. farm wife and mother of 12 children
f. the married Creighton son; father of two boys
g. storekeeper who seeks vengeance on the town ruffian
h. farmer and respected town leader
i. cousin who deserts the Union army but later returns
j. neighbor who helps protect the youngest Creighton son
k. young wife who feels like an outsider to the family until the war begins
l. young man killed at Pittsburg Landing
m. town ruffian who burns the Creighton barn
n. schoolteacher and Union soldier

True or False:

Answer T for true or F for false in the blanks below.

_____1. The Creighton family is hated because of an ancestor's criminal past.
_____2. Abraham Lincoln sends a letter to Jethro Creighton.
_____3. Jethro never really feels comfortable around Nancy.
_____4. Bill Creighton dies in the war.
_____5. Jethro wants to improve his mind by reading and studying.

Short Answer:

On a seperate piece of paper, write a brief response to each prompt.

1. Tell about two ways in which the main character of the story needs to grow up quickly.
2. Name three things that are different for the Creightons before the war and after it.
3. Explain how the mercy shown to Travis Burdow is repaid.

Essay:

Respond to the following on the back of this paper. *Across Five Aprils* shows the reader several points of view from both sides of the Civil War. Having read the book and learned about the different characters' perceptions of the war, what side (if any) do you think was in the right? Do you feel the outcome of the war was just? Defend your answers by showing your reasoning and providing facts wherever relevant.

Interpretation

Explain the meaning of these quotations from *Across Five Aprils*.

Chapter 1   "One didn't talk about such things; the world, she knew, was impatient with women who value their own children too highly."

Chapter 1   "It was not a behavior pattern of which the backwoods community approved; a lot of people smirked a little when they mentioned Bill Creighton."

Chapter 1   "And Bill, for the first time that John could remember, had reservations about a subject and seemed unwilling to discuss it with his brother."

Chapter 2   "What I want us to answer in this year of 1861 is this, John: Does the trouble over slavery come because men's hearts is purer above the Mason-Dixon line? Or does slavery throw a shadder over greed and keep that greed from showin' up quite so bare and ugly?"

Chapter 2   "There is an awakenin' inside us of human decency and responsibility. If I didn't believe that, I wouldn't grieve fer the children I've buried; I wouldn't look for'ard to the manhood of this youngest one."

Chapter 3   "They say, too, that hundreds of people climbed up on rooftops to watch the fight— as if it was a circus of some kind."

Chapter 3   "I don't know if anybody ever 'wins' a war, Jeth. I think that the beginnin's of this war has been fanned by hate till it's a blaze now; and a blaze kin destroy him that makes it and him that the fire was set to hurt."

Chapter 4   "It seemed strange that this scrap of paper had actually come from a battlefield, that Tom's big hand had actually touched it."

Chapter 4   "The hardships one endured had a purpose; his mother had been careful to make him aware of that."

Chapter 4   ". . . but you remember, Jeth, that it took far more courage for Bill to do what he did than it does for John and me to carry out our plans next week."

Chapter 5   "My Pa don't teach me one way or the other. He knows that I think more of my brother than anybody else in the world—no matter where he is."

Chapter 5   "I didn't tell you this, but in the store this mornin' there was a man named Guy Wortman. And there was another man, Trav Burdow's pa—"

Chapter 6   "If someone had asked Jethro to name a time when he left childhood behind him, he might have named that last week of March in 1862."

Chapter 7   "Men from all over the county came to Matt Creighton's aid that spring."

Chapter 7   "Has justice been done, Gentlemen? Has an ailing man who commands the respect of those in his county who recognize integrity—has this man suffered enough to satisfy your patriotic zeal?"

Chapter 9   "The deserters came in droves."

Chapter 9   "Yes, I reckon it's Eb—what there's left of him."

Chapter 9   "Ol' Abe. Mr. Lincoln. Mr. President."

Chapter 11   "Ma—Bill wants that I shood tell you this—he was not at Pittsburg Landing. That bullet was not fired by him . . . "

Chapter 12   "What is this goin' to do to an eighteen-year-old boy, Matt? Kin a lad come through weeks of this kind of actions without becomin' a hardened man?"

Chapter 12   "Don't build me up too much, Shad. Somethin's like to break inside of me."

Application

Take what you know about *Across Five Aprils* and use it to respond to either a writing or a drawing activity.

Writing:

Work in size-appropriate groups to write and perform the conversations that might have occurred in one of the following situations.

- Matt and Ellen meet for the first time. (2 persons)
- Jenny and Shad meet for the first time after Shad has been wounded. (2 persons)
- Bill returns to the Creighton home after the war. (number of persons can vary)
- Bill and Jethro see one another after the war. (2 persons)
- Dave Burdow and Matt Creighton talk about their past and their future. (2 persons)
- The newlyweds, Shad and Jenny, visit Matt, Ellen, and Jethro. (5 persons)
- Jethro and Ross Milton visit Shad and Jenny after the war. (4 persons)
- Jethro, now a grown man, tells stories of the Civil War to his nephews. (3 persons)
- John returns home to Nancy and his sons. (4 persons)
- John returns home to Ellen and Matt. (3 persons)
- Jethro and Shad meet after the war to talk about the future. (2 persons)
- Tom, Eb, Shad, and John meet during the war to talk about their experiences. (4 persons)

Drawing:

Choose one of the following activities and draw your response to it on the back of this paper.

- Draw Jethro at the beginning of the book, the middle, and again at the end.
- Make a drawing of your favorite part of the book.
- Draw what you see as the most important part of the book.
- Illustrate some of the things that Jethro learns during the course of the book.
- Draw Jethro as he might look 10 years after the book ends.
- Draw Jethro meeting with Bill after the war.
- Make a drawing of some people Jethro would think of as heroic.
- Draw the most climactic point in the book.
- Illustrate the home that Jenny and Shad make together.
- Illustrate the home that Jethro grows up to have.

Bibliography of Related Reading

Nonfiction

Archer, Jules. *A House Divided: The Lives of Ulysses S. Grant and Robert E. Lee.* Scholastic, 1995.

Carratello, John and Patty. *Thematic Unit: Civil War.* Teacher Created Materials, 1991.

Carter, Alden R. *The Battle of Gettysburg.* F. Watts, 1991.

Cooper, Michael L. *From Slave to Civil War Hero.* Lodestar Books, 1994.

Denney, Robert E. *Civil War Medicine: Care and Comfort to the Wounded.* Sterling Publications, 1994.

Elish, Dan. *Harriet Tubman and the Underground Railroad.* Millbrook Press, 1993.

Freedman, Russell. *Lincoln: A Photobiography.* Clarion, 1987.

Garrison, Webb B. *Civil War Trivia and Fact Book.* Rutledge Hill Press, 1992.

Gowan, Hugh and Judy. *Blue and Grey Cookery.* Daisy Publishing, 1980 (Call: 800-356-7622)

Katz, William Loren. *An Album of the Civil War.* Franklin Watts, Inc., 1974.

Lester, Julius. *To Be a Slave.* Scholastic, 1968.

Massey, Mary Elizabeth. *Women in the Civil War.* University of Nebraska Press, 1994.

Miers, Earl S. *Billy Yank and Johnny Reb: How They Fought and Made Up.* Rand, 1959.

Moore, Kay. *If You Lived at the Time of the Civil War.* Scholastic, Inc., 1994.

Pleasant Company staff. *Addy's Cookbook: A Peek at Dining in the Past With Meals You Can Cook Today.* Pleasant Company, 1994.

Rappaport, Doreen. *Escape from Slavery: Five Journeys to Freedom.* HarperCollins, 1991.

Ray, Delia. *Behind the Blue and Gray: A Soldier's Life in the Civil War.* Lodestar Books, 1991.

Reit, Seymour. *Behind Rebel Lives: The Incredible Story of Emma Edmonds.* Harcourt Brace Jovanovich, 1991.

Rhea, Gordon C. *The Battle of the Wilderness.* Louisiana State University Press, 1994.

Steins, Richard. *The Nation Divides: The Civil War, 1820–1880.* Twenty-First Century Books, 1993.

Stevens, Bryna. *Frank Thompson: Her Civil War Story.* Maxwell Macmillan International, 1992.

Tracey, Patrick Austin. *Military Leaders of the Civil War.* facts on File, 1993.

Wade, Linda. *Andersonville: A Civil War Tragedy.* Rourke Enterprise, 1991.

Ward, Geoffrey C. *The Civil War: An Illustrated History.* Alfred A. Knopf, Inc., 1990.

Werstein, Irving. *The Many Faces of the Civil War.* Messner, 1961.

Fiction

Alphin, Elaine Marie. *The Ghost Cadet.* Henry Holt and Co., 1991.

Beatty, Patricia. *Charley Skedaddle.* Morrow Junior Books, 1987.

———. *Be Ever Hopeful, Hannalee.* Morrow Junior Books, 1988.

———. *Who Comes with Cannons?* Morrow Junior Books, 1992.

Crane, Stephen. *The Red Badge of Courage.* Watermill, 1981.

Forman, James D. *Becca's Story.* C Scribner's Sons, 1992.

Gaugh, Patricia Lee. *Thunder at Gettysburg.* Putnam, 1990.

Hamilton, Virginia. *The House of Dies Drear.* Collier, 1984.

Hansen, Joyce. *Out from This Place.* Avon, 1992.

———. *Which Way to Freedom?* Avon, 1992.

Houston, Gloria. *Mountain Valor.* Philomel Books, 1994

Keith, Harold. *Rifles for Watie.* Harper & Row, 1987.

Lyon, George Ella. *Here and Then.* Orchard Books, 1994.

Nixon, Joan Lowery. *A Dangerous Promise.* Delacorte, 1994.

Paulsen, Gary. *Culpepper's Cannon.* Dell, 1992.

Porter, Connie Rose. *Meet Addy: An American Girl.* Pleasant Company, 1993.

Reeder, Carolyn. *Shades of Gray.* Collier Macmillan, 1989.

Shura, Mary Francis. *Gentle Annie: The True Story of a Civil War Nurse.* Scholastic, 1991.

Smucker, Barbara. *Runaway to Freedom.* Harper & Row, 1977.

Winter, Jeanette. *Follow the Drinking Gourd.* Alfred A. Knopf, Inc., 1988.

Wisler, G. Clifton. *Red Cap.* Lodestar Books, 1991.

Video

The Civil War (an eleven-part PBS series)
Write: PBS Video, 1320 Braddock Place, Alexandria, VA 22314; Call: 1-800-424-7963.

Music

Currie, Stephen. *Music in the Civil War.* Betterway Books, 1992.

Moore, Frank. *The Civil War in Song & Story.* Gordon Press, 1980.

Silverman, Jerry. *Songs of the American People.* Mel Bay Publications, 1993.

Answer Key

Page 10

1. Jethro is nine years old with blond hair and blue eyes. He is intelligent with "special talents."
2. The story takes place on a farm in southern Illinois.
3. The characters are Ellen, Matt, John, Nancy, Bill, Tom, and Jenny Creighton; Eb (Carron); Shadrach Yale; and Wilse Graham. Descriptions will vary.
4. Eb is Matt Creighton's nephew. He was orphaned as a young boy and came to live with the Creighton family.
5. Bill and John are brothers, close in age and the best of friends. Although their natures are different, they share a strong bond that seems inseparable.
6. Jenny and Shadrach have been sweethearts and would still like to be. Jenny's father, however, feels that Jenny is too young for such a relationship.
7. Cousin Wilse Graham says that he cannot justify to God, the keeping of slaves but since people have kept slaves throughout history, and since the founding fathers accepted slavery, he insists that slavery is justifiable.
8. Shad tells the Creightons that the Confederates have opened fire on Fort Sumter, thereby beginning the war.
9. At first Jethro is caught up in the excitement of the other boys and in the tales of heroism in war, but when war becomes a reality, Jethro becomes scared and worried. War no longer seems exciting and glorious.
10. Bill fights with the South because he believes that Congress favors the North and that the North oppresses the South. He objects to slavery, but he believes the greater fault is with the North.

Page 12

Note: The following answers are only suggested. The students' answers may vary. Accept any reasonable translations, including idiomatic changes.

I. 1. Your hopes are making you unreasonable, Jethro.
   2. It amazes me, Jethro, it does for a fact, the way you can recollect all the things Shadrach tells you and change them from his way of talking into mine.
   3. Are you exhausted, Jethro?
   4. I have a crock of lettuce for you, Jethro, although I am being terribly wasteful by picking it too early.
   5. As much as I care for my family, a crowded cabin bothers me; it always has.

II. Responses will vary.

Page 13

1. h) Abraham Lincoln wins the presidential election of 1860.
2. c) South Carolina passes an order of secession.
3. a) Major Robert Anderson moves his garrison to Fort Sumter in the Charleston Harbor.
4. d) Governor Francis Pickens demands that the Union surrender Fort Sumter.
5. i) The *Star of the West*, a Union ship, attempts to deliver reinforcements and supplies to Fort Sumter. It is fired upon and leaves.
6. b) Six more states secede and Lincoln takes office. Fort Sumter remains one of two Southern forts under Union control.
7. j) Lincoln orders an attempt for provisions to be sent to Fort Sumter, where soldiers are in danger of starvation.
8. f) The Confederates at Fort Johnson fire on the Union soldiers in Fort Sumter.
9. k) All Northern and Southern negotiations cease.
10. g) Major Anderson surrenders.
11. e) The United States declares war on the Confederacy.

Page 15

1. Grant has overtaken Forts Henry and Donelson. These are the first major victories for the North, and they are debilitating to the South.
2. Tom has become disillusioned with the glory of war, and he is hoping to convert Jethro as well.

Answer Key *(cont.)*

3. Ellen allows Jethro to bring the letter to Shad's home, visit with Shad, and spend the night there.
4. Ellen considers her dependency on coffee a weakness.
5. Jethro meets Jake Roscoe who asks Jethro to bring him a newspaper from town.
6. Sam Gardiner gives Jethro a handful of gumdrops.
7. Ross Milton is the editor of the local paper. He defends Jethro and the Creightons at the town store, buys Jethro dinner, and gives him a book on grammar. (Allow students to provide any or all of the listed answers.)
8. Jethro says that he thinks better of his brother than anyone else, no matter what.
9. Dave Burdow protects Jethro from Guy Wortman who is lying in wait for Jethro to pass.
10. Accept any reasonable response.

Extra Credit: The phrase is a translation from *Julius Caesar* by William Shakespeare (Act III, Scene 1; "Et tu, Brute."). It alludes to the betrayal of Caesar by Brutus, Caesar's friend. Shad is pointing out Jethro's seeming betrayal; however, his comment is ironic.

Page 18

- ● —Fort Donelson
- ☆ —Fort Henry
- ∿∿ —Mississippi River
- ∿ —Tennessee River
- —Ohio River
- ∿ —Cumberland River

Page 20

1. Matt Creighton suffers a debilitating sickness, perhaps a heart attack, that weakens his body and instincts. The care of the farm is left to Jethro, who must become the "man of the family."
2. Jenny receives a love letter from Shad which she does not wish to share with the family. Jethro is angry because all news is precious and letters to the family have always been shared. It seems he also feels a bit jealous.
3. Nancy tells Jethro about the significance of love letters and that when he is old enough to receive one, he will want to keep the words for himself as well. She also says that such words should not be shared because that would betray the writer.
4. They throw down a corded stack of switches.
5. The ruffians burn down the Creighton barn with all its farm equipment, hay, and grain, and they throw coal oil down their well.
6. Dan Lawrence tells the family of Tom's death at Pittsburg Landing.
7. Jethro was named for a respected, local doctor.
8. The Creighton's record their family dates in their Bible.
9. The oldest son moved to California many years ago during the Gold Rush and has never been heard from since. The two oldest daughters married and moved to Ohio.
10. Sam Gardiner lets Guy Wortman know that he will be out of town for a week. Instead, he hides out in his own store, and when Wortman comes in to vandalize the place, Gardiner shoots him in the backside with buckshot. Wortman becomes publicly humiliated as well as indisposed due to his embarrassing injury.

Page 25

1. Dave Burdow sends a load of logs for the new barn.
2. Shad writes that General McClellan is missing a coldness, tenacity, and "singleness of purpose" that the winner of the war must

Answer Key *(cont.)*

have.

3. Thousands of soldiers had begun to desert the army. They are sick of fighting and troubled by the grim state of things for the Union Army.

4. Point Prospect is a camp where many deserters are hiding. It is dangerous because the deserters are angry, scared, and anxious, and therefore willing to do anything to protect themselves. Even the Federal Registrars are afraid to go there.

5. A man avoids the draft by hiring a substitute for three hundred dollars to take his place.

6. Hig Phillips is murdered by a group of deserters who resent his draft dodging while others have fought in the war for more than two years.

7. The Federal Registrars come looking for Eb, who has deserted the Union Army.

8. Jethro discovers Eb hiding in the woods.

9. Jethro writes a letter to President Lincoln, asking for his advice on Eb's desertion.

10. Lincoln tells Jethro that all deserters who willingly return by April 1 will be returned to their posts without punishment other than loss of pay for the time they were gone.

Page 28

1. 600 square feet
2. 6,000 cubic feet
3. 616 square feet
4. 9,856 cubic feet
5. 15 feet
6. 18 feet

Page 30

1. Shad is wounded and nearly dies.
2. Jenny marries Shad on August 14, 1863.
3. President Lincoln offers a full pardon to any Confederate who pledges loyalty to the Union. He also offers the return to the Union of any Confederate state with 10 percent of the population voting to rejoin.
4. Shad sends letters to Jethro, specifically addressed to him.
5. John meets Bill in the rebel prison camp. The two exchange news and reconnect as brothers.

6. Bill relays the message that he was never at Pittsburg Landing, so it could not have been him who killed Tom.

7. Ed Turner is afraid his son is going to become hardened or changed in a terrible way by seeing—and possibly taking part in—the crimes against Southern citizens.

8. Ross Milton believes it will be very difficult for the freed people to survive because they do not have the education and skills necessary for survival. He also believes that most of the people fighting for their freedom will not do anything to help them to survive and succeed.

9. Jethro is devastated by the news that Abraham Lincoln was shot and killed on that date.

10. Shad promises to take Jethro with him and Jenny so that Jethro can receive a good education.

Page 33

1. 29%
2. 53% to 60%
3.–6. Answers will vary according to the reference source. There are no definitive numbers.

Page 42

1. b	11. m
2. h	12. f
3. e	13. l
4. a	14. g
5. n	1. F
6. j	2. T
7. c	3. F
8. i	4. F
9. k	5. T
10. d	

Short Answer and Essay: Responses will vary.

Page 43

Responses will vary.

Page 44

Conversations and drawings will vary.